VEDANTA, PLATO, AND KANT

PAUL DEUSSEN

TRANSLATED BY

ALEXANDER JACOB

978-0-6452126-2-4

Vedanta, Plato, and Kant
Paul Deussen
Translated by Alexander Jacob

MANTICORE PRESS
WWW.MANTICORE.PRESS

CONTENTS

Alexander Jacob

Paul Deussen (1845-1919) began his studies in theology and philosophy in Bonn. Later he studied Sanskrit in Bonn and Berlin and classical philology in Berlin and Marburg, where he did his dissertation on Plato's *Sophist* in 1869. Deussen became an ardent admirer of the German philosopher Arthur Schopenhauer (1788-1860) and the philosophy of Immanuel Kant (1724-1804). He founded the Schopenhauer Gesellschaft in 1911, edited the *Schopenhauer Jahrbuch* from 1912, and worked on an edition of Schopenhauer's works. He was also a friend of Friedrich Nietzsche in Bonn and wrote about his friendship with him in his *Erinnerungen an Nietzsche* (1901). Unlike Deussen, however, Nietzsche had little interest in the Idealistic Upanishadic philosophy preferring the hierarchical sociology of the *Laws of Manu* instead in his late works.

Deussen's first publication was *Elemente der Metaphysik* (1877). This was followed by *Das System des Vedânta. Nach den Brahma-Sûtra's des Bâdarâyana und dem Commentare des* Çankara (1883) and *Die Sûtra's des Vedânta oder die* Çariraka-Mimansa *des Badarayana nebst einem vollständigen Kommentare des* Çankara (1887). Then, between 1894 and 1917, he produced a history of philosophy, *Allgemeine Geschichte der Philosophie* in seven volumes. He also published a translation of *Sechzig Upanishad's des Veda* in 1897. His visit to India in 1904 was recorded in his *Erinnerungen an Indien* (1904). His effort to show the resemblances between the Idealistic philosophies of India, Greece and Germany produced two pamphlets *Vedânta und Platonismus im Lichte der Kantischen Philosophie* (1904) and the present work *Vedânta, Platonismus und Kant* in 1917.[1]

The present work is mainly a defense of Shankara's Advaita Vedānta philosophy as well as an elucidation of the Greek Idealistic doctrines of Parmenides and Plato. In all these schools of thought, Deussen detects a similar basic understanding of the world as a mere appearance distinct from Ideal Reality. He approximated this understanding to the Kantian notion of 'things in themselves' (*Dinge-an-sich)* and noted a degeneration of the original Vedic and Upanishadic worldview in the philosophies that followed, such as the Sāmkhya and Buddhism, just as there was a corruption of Parmenides' doctrine of Being in the philosophy of his pupil Zeno. Similarly, he believes that Kant's revolutionary Idealistic insights in Germany were also distorted by the post-Kantian thinkers and not generally understood in their original form except by Arthur Schopenhauer (1788-1860), who developed the doctrine of the world as a mere representation produced by the innate intuitive forms within the Intellect – Space, Time, and Causality. The Reality of the world itself is, according to Schopenhauer, constituted of the Will, which manifests itself in all creatures as individual wills

---

[1] *Vedânta, Platonismus und Kant,* Vienna: Urania Bücherei, 1917.

or egos. Therefore, redemption from this world of strife can only be achieved by knowledge of the unreality of the empirical world and an abjuration of the Will in us that binds us to the fateful vicissitudes of an egoistic life.

As regards Deussen's assessment of the development of philosophical schools in ancient India and Greece, it is true that the Upanishads, which are the philosophical part of Vedic literature, were indeed revived in a pure form in the 8th century A.D. by Shankara in his non-dualistic Advaita Vedānta philosophy. But Deussen's denunciation of the Sāmkhya system as dualistic Realism is indefensible since its concentration on the two principles of Purusha as Pure Consciousness and the Prakriti as Matter is the same as the Idealistic distinction between Being and Becoming in ancient Greece or modern Germany. The Sāmkhya system of the universe is also much more elaborate than the purely metaphysical concerns of either the Upanishads or Advaita Vedānta. It adeptly explains the process of infusion of the Intellect into matter as individual intellects, egos, and minds followed by the sense organs of action and the five senses. In the macrocosm and microcosm, the mundane elements of earth, water, fire, air, and ether finally appear.[2] The three *gunas* — *sattva* (ethereal and illuminating), *rajas* (restless and mobile), and *tamas* (heavy and inert) — or the modes that characterize all matter, also provide an efficient moral measure of the value of the manifest world. Even though Sāmkhya does not dismiss the empirical world as an illusion as the Vedānta does, its stress on liberation

---

[2] See *The Sánkhya Aphorisms of Kapila*, tr. James R. Ballantyne, London, 1885, *The Sāmkhya Kārikā* [of] *Iśvara Kṛṣṇa ... with the Commentary of Gaudapādācārya*, tr. Har Dutt Sharma, Poona, 1933; cf. Gerald James Larson, *Classical Sāmkhya: An Interpretation of its History and Meaning*, Delhi, 1969.

VEDANTA, PLATO, AND KANT

There is one thought — it can perhaps be called the most important that mankind possesses since on it are based religion, philosophy, as well as art within its total possibility — a thought that is found expressed, sometimes obscurely sometimes clearly, everywhere that the human mind has attained a clearer consciousness of its own nature but has not found a clearer expression than in the Kantian philosophy, where it is clothed in the simple formula:

'The world is an appearance, not a thing in itself.'

The world, the entire world, such as it extends around us in an immeasurable manner in infinite Space, and not less the unfathomable abundance of feelings, strivings, and imaginations that appear to us from our own inner Self, all of that is only an appearance, only the form that Being assumes in order to be represented in a consciousness such as ours but not the form in which the things in themselves, independent of our consciousness, may exist according to their ultimate, deepest, and innermost nature. On this thought as its conscious or unconscious precondition are based — as mentioned — all religions, every deeply penetrating philosophy, indeed also all art that is in the fullest sense worthy of its name. Before we demonstrate this, it will be useful to consider in greater detail the mentioned thought of Kantian philosophy in its origin and significance.

The philosophy of the Middle Ages had dealt with two great obscure problems, the question about the immortality of the soul and that about the existence of an otherworldly God. The philosophy of Descartes is, in the main, nothing but a clear, logical analysis of these basic views of the Middle Ages. For that very reason their scientific untenability was made apparent. The ancient holy relics that appeared very impressive and respectable in the doctrinal system of an Albert Magnus and Thomas Aquinas, just as in the twilit medieval cathedral, had to appear very spurious and decayed when Descartes drew them into the bright sunlight of a scientific observation. He believed that he had with his demonstration of the existence of God and the immortality of the soul rendered a good service to the Church, but the Church judged otherwise; it had condemned his doctrines already a few years after the death of their author, the Protestant Church at the Synod of Dortrecht (1656) and by placing the writings of Descartes on the Papal Index (1663). But it was too late; the movement had already begun its progress and could no longer be held back. How did the immaterial spiritual substance relate to the body enclosing it? How the otherworldly God to the world created by Him? These questions occupied the following century and led, after many strifes and vicissitudes, to the Pantheism of Spinoza, to the Idealism of Leibniz and Berkeley, to the Skepticism of Hume, and finally to French Materialism which, as the herald of the French Revolution, together with the latter itself, threatened to flood the world from France.

In the midst of the distractedness of the philosophical situation occurs the appearance of Kant. With fine and eloquent words he describes in the first foreword to his masterpiece, the *Critique of Pure Reason*,[5] the anarchy that had burst and complains about it that, in spite of all efforts, no certain knowledge had been acquired about the most important of all questions, about God, freedom, and immortality, and poses the very justified question whether the human mind indeed possesses the organs and powers to create a scientifically based conviction on such transcendental problems that go beyond all experience. In order to determine this, he subjects human reason and, in a broader sense, the entire human intellect to a critical investigation which he calls transcendental, because it wishes to test the justification of the philosophizing hitherto. The result of this test was predictable. With wonderful objectivity, he lays out the entire machinery of the intellectual apparatus and shows how all its organs and functions are unmistakably determined and capable only of recording and processing experiential material just as they wander in a void and lose all significance as soon as we undertake to go beyond the experiential world with our intellectual powers. So far, therefore, the result of the critique of pure reason with all its deeply penetrating investigations was a merely negative one. But by taking apart the human intellect like a clockwork and revealing and describing all its innate powers, sense-boundedness, understanding, and reason, individually he made, to his own and the world's surprise, the greatest discovery that the entire history of philosophy has recorded because in his investigations it was demonstrated that certain essential constituents of the Reality surrounding us prove to be innate intuitional forms of our intellect. These basic

---

[5] [*The Critique of Pure Reason* was first published in 1781.] [All notes in box-brackets are by the translator.]

elements of the entire empirical Reality which are proven by Kant as original functions innate in the consciousness are, first, the endless all-encompassing Space, secondly the equally endless Time in which all worldly events take place, and thirdly and lastly, the only one of the twelve categories established by Kant[6] that may be maintained, Causality, that is, the nexus of Causality that connects together all events as causes and effects. These three essential elements of the world pervading, sustaining, and regulating the entire universe according to law, Space, Time, and Causality are not, as we are naturally inclined to believe, objective substances that are independent of us, but they are, as Kant and the great perfecter of his doctrine, Schopenhauer,[7] have proved in a manner that has not been disputed and is indisputable, subjective forms of intuition innate in the general consciousness of the universe and realizing itself in every individual consciousness as brain functions. This is and remains the fundamental truth of all philosophy. The proofs for this we have brought forth elsewhere (*Elements of Metaphysics*, Arts. 48-68); here, only the consequences of these proofs should occupy us and, first, in relation to religion.

The highest assets of religion, the most valuable consolations that it has to offer, can be summarized in three words: God, immortality, and freedom. These three

---

[6] [In the *Critique of Pure Reason* Kant postulated the following 12 *a priori* categories as innate in the mind: unity, plurality, and totality for concept of *quantity;* reality, negation, and limitation for the concept of *quality;* inherence and subsistence, cause and effect, and community for the *concept of relation;* and possibility-impossibility, existence-nonexistence, and necessity-contingency for the *concept of modality.* In addition to these categories Kant posited the two intellectual forms of intutions, space and time.]

[7] [Schopehauer's masterwork *The World as Will and Representation* was first published in 1818 and expanded into two volumes in 1844.]

aids to salvation can be maintained only if Kant is right, if Space, Time, and Causality are only subjective forms of perception, and, therefore, the entire universe extended in Space and Time and governed by Causality is only an appearance, not a thing in itself. For, if it is posited that the world order surrounding us were an eternal ordering of things in themselves independent of our consciousness, then God, immortality, and freedom would cease to be valid, and all religion must be borne to its grave.

Man's perspicacity has long striven to prove the existence of God. Then, when man recognized the futility of these attempts, he consoled himself with the fact that its opposite too could not be proven. But the truth is that maintaining the Reality of the world independent of consciousness from the anti-Kantian standpoint produces the non-existence of God as an inevitable consequence. Around us on all sides, Space stretches into infinity. Outside this, there can be no existence because such a thing would be at no place and, therefore, nowhere and consequently not at all. Therefore everything that exists, in general, must exist within Space, but in it, there exists only that which fills some space and that we call matter. It is, according to its most accurate definition, 'that which fills a space.' Consequently, there can be in the entire infinite Space, in all near and distant locations, in the heavens and on earth, nothing but matter. Materialism is, from the empirical point of view, the only possible, true and logical worldview. In the infinite Space, partly empty, partly filled with bodies, there is no place for God. Only the Kantian doctrine, that the entire infinite Space with all that it contains is only an appearance, only an imagination in our consciousness comparable to a dream image, raises us above this desolate view, and thereby place is again made for another otherworldly divine reality, even though we cannot grasp such with our intellect which is bound to spatial appearances. Just as Space excludes the existence of God, Time too makes it impossible for us to adhere to the immortality of the soul. Like everything else, our existence also proceeds in Time. It has a beginning in Time through conception and birth and finds its end in Time through death, and this end is an absolute just as that beginning was. After our death, we will be no more and no less than what we were before our existence; empirically considered, after hundred years, we will be the same that we were before hundred years, thus nothing. It is different only if we understand, with Kant, Time as a mere subjective form of intuition bound to our intellect. Only for the latter is our existence extended in Time, our life in itself, however, is timeless, is raised above beginning and end, above birth and death, and therewith immortal.

Just as God and immortality are excluded by the subjectivity of Space and Time, so is the third element of salvation of religion, the freedom of the will serving as a precondition of all morality excluded by the unlimited rule of the law of Causality and made possible once again through Kant's great doctrine that all our activities must be incorporated into the network of causes and effects only for the intellectual observation but that with this physical lack of freedom in any one activity there exists its metaphysical freedom, even though we can understand the latter very little.

We have shown that the fundamental doctrines of Kant serve as an indispensable precondition for all religion. By that, we do not understand that only with Kant was religion made possible in the world but rather that the Kantian fundamental idea existed long before Kant and that all religious minds at all times silently presupposed unconsciously or half-consciously the great truth that, however, was raised to scientific evidence only through Kant's proofs.

Like religion, all philosophy is rooted in that which was raised in Kant's doctrine to its fundamental dogma, and the philosophy of all countries and ages is fundamentally nothing but a search for a principle for the explanation of the universe, for that secretly hidden core that appears before our eyes as this spatial and temporal extension of the universe, in short, and in Kant's words, all philosophy is a search for the thing-in-itself.

We intend to prove this claim in greater detail at the two high points that philosophy scaled in ancient times, Vedānta and Platonism, and wish, before we proceed to that, to recall just briefly that, besides religion and philosophy, a third, extremely fine bloom of the tree of mankind, art in all its forms, has always had the Kantian principles as an unconscious precondition. An artist is an unconscious metaphysician; he does not shape according to empirical Reality but goes beyond it; he attempts to capture the Eternal that manifests itself in all the forms and events of this world and, by representing this in shapes, colors, words, and tones, he offers us a revelation of the inner essence of things that defers to the religious and philosophical revelation, and complements it in an efficient way. The Kantian worldview, which always underlay all religion, philosophy, and art, could not have been the eternal truth if it did not emerge more or less clearly everywhere that the human mind penetrated into the depths, as this occurred, for example, in India through the Upanishads of the Vedas and the Vedānta based on them and in Greece through Parmenides and Plato. To consider both these phenomena in the light of the Kantian philosophy is the task that we have set ourselves here.

*****

The development of Indian culture and, with it, Indian religion and philosophy is broken up naturally into three periods, the ancient Vedic, the later Vedic, and the post-Vedic, of which the first may be allotted roughly to 1000 B.C., the second from that time to 500 B.C. There cannot be more precise determinations since the Indians were always too devoted to eternal interests for them to be able to worry about external historiography, chronology, etc. As a substitute for the lack of firm dates, we have in India a continuous development before us that proceeds in a series of phases organically growing out of each other and presents the great drama of a worldview that rises in stages from childish beginnings to the highest perfection.

In the hymns of the *Rigveda* originating from the ancient Vedic age, this oldest book that India and perhaps the world in general possesses, we observe as a general view a richly developed polytheism whose gods are still almost completely transparent personifications of natural forces and natural phenomena. Thus Varuna, to mention only the most important phenomena, is the starry sky, Usha the dawn, Sūrya, Savitar, Mitra, Vishnu, and Pūshan the sun, Vāyu or Vāta the wind, Indra the storm, Rudra the blazing lightning, Parjanya the rain and Agni the fire so close to man, in its effects so beneficent and yet so frightful. All the phenomena of Nature, we can in this manner summarize the philosophy of the *Rigveda*, are the effects of super-powerful beings but like humans and characterized by human weaknesses to whom one can speak, whom one can influence through sacrifices and prayers, that is, through gifts and flattery, and direct according to one's Will.

This childish view is broken through already on the ground of the *Rigveda* itself. In the latest hymns of this incomparable book, we see breaking through, on the one hand, doubts and occasionally open mockery of the divine world and, on the other, hand in hand with it, a deeper philosophical view shining forth. We glimpse a characteristic search for, and questioning about, the eternal One that lies at the basis of all the multiplicity of gods, worlds, and beings. Here, as in Greece, the first step to philosophy is the recognition of the unity of all Being that finds its wonderful expression in some hymns, of which we wish to cite one (X,129):

1. At that time there was not non-existence nor existence,
    No space of air, no heavens above,
    Who preserved the world, who enclosed it?
    Where was the deep Abyss, where the Ocean?

2. Then there was no death nor immortality,
    Nor night nor day was apparent,
    The One breathed without wind in the beginning,
    Besides it, there was nothing.

3. The entire universe was covered in darkness
    An Ocean without light, lost in night.

> That which was hidden in the balance
> Was born through the force of Fire

4. From this there arose, first born,
    As the kernel of knowledge, Love,
    The wise men, seeking, found the root of existence
    In non-existence, in the impulse of the heart.

5. When they spread their measuring cord through
    What was there underneath? and what above?
    Carriers of germs, forces that stirred,
    Self-establishment below, tension above.

6. Yet who has succeeded in searching,
    Who has investigated whence the creation originated?
    The gods have sprung here from it!
    So who can say whence they come?

7.   He who brought forth the creation
    Who looks upon it in the light of highest heaven
    The one who has produced it or not produced it
    He knows ! – or perhaps he too does not know ?

The brilliance of this primeval piece of deep philosophy cannot be reproduced even only approximately through any translation. But even in it, if not the artistic perfection, still the high philosophical clear-sightedness is recognizable that penetrates deeper and deeper from verse 1 to 4, half withholding its expression repeatedly in the consciousness of its inadequacy until the poet, towards the end, is seized more and more by cold doubt about the possibility of fathoming the final secret of existence. Another hymn (I, 164) summarizes the same knowledge of the One in the short words: '*ekam sad viprā bahudhā vadanti.* The poets call manifold what is only One.'

In this thought lies the kernel of all of philosophy. A multiplicity is every positing of one thing outside another in Space, every positing of one thing after another in Time, every mutual conditioning of causes and effects, and one who denies multiplicity to true Reality has also unconsciously denied Space, Time, and Causality since all three cease at the same time as multiplicity.

After man came to the recognition of the unity of Being, it had to be the next task to determine more closely this unity. Many attempts emerged in the following late Vedic period to understand that One, the Eternal, the Unchangeable, as Prajāpati, as Purusha, as Brahman until one found the One where alone it is to be found, namely, in our own inner Self. Here one grasped the unmoving pole in the flow of appearances and designated it as Brahman, which means actually a 'prayer,' that is, as the raising of the mind above the individual existence as is felt during prayer, at the moment of religious meditation, or, synonymous with it, but more striking philosophically, as the ātman, the Self, that is, as that which constitutes, in contrast to everything that comes and goes, to everything that becomes and is changeable, our true, deepest and independent Being, our actual Self and, with it, the Self of the entire universe.

The later Vedic period (roughly from 1000 B.C. to 500 B.C.) to which this intellectual development belongs brought forth, along with the Brāhmanas, those gigantic ritual texts of Indian antiquity, a series of religio-philosophical documents that, since they tend to form the final chapter of the Vedas, are called Vedānta (i.e., the end of the Vedas) or Upanishads (secret knowledge) and are to be considered the finest bloom of ancient Indian wisdom, as the most valuable legacy that mankind owes to this unique people. There are two basic concepts around which all ideas of the Upanishads move, the Brahman and the ātman. Both are regularly used as completely synonymous; where a difference can be recognized there, Brahman signifies the principle insofar as it is realized in the universe, ātman the same in man. Both the Upanishads contain a colorful multiplicity of legends, allegories, and reflections in which many thought they found only a chaos of conflicting opinions until we succeeded recently in determining the age of the Upanishads compared to one another and in recognizing in them a historical development whose fundamental features we wish to cite from our *General History of Philosophy* (Vol. I, Part 2). First, however, we must make a general observation.

One who is today still of the opinion that the principal sources of the thought of a philosopher are to be sought in the doctrines of his predecessors and that the newly emergent system is, as it were, added and subtracted through continuation, modification, and combination of the earlier dogmas will be inclined to consider the later doctrinal system as more perfect than the earlier. The situation is often represented conversely to one who has understood that the philosopher is inspired first not by the doctrinal views of his predecessors but by the immediate view of the nature of things extended in himself and around him and that every great progress in philosophy is based on an immediate *aperçu*, on a perception and internalization of a hitherto concealed fact of Reality. The view obtained in this manner tends then to be increasingly distorted and corrupted by inferior successors as it passes from hand to hand, that is, through the fact that one forces metaphysical truths into the template of the physical manner of viewing that is alone comprehensible to the common man and is thereby disfigured until once again a genuine metaphysician appears in the world, like a rare phoenix, pushes aside all those useless intermediate stages and grasps the original view corrupted by them in its full profundity and, similarly inspired by the Nature that conducted those great predecessors, shapes it further in a congenial manner. A shining example of this corruption and the final return to the misunderstood original is offered in recent times by the way in which Schopenhauer discarded the speculation of the post-Kantian imitators and, partly correcting partly completing, returned to Kant. The same process of a brilliant original creation, a misapprehending continuation, and a final reestablishment and correct development of the original we will meet in India as well as in Greece.

So in the Upanishads, first, the oldest is also the best. It consists mainly of narratives and speeches that are related in the *Brihadāranyaka Upanishad* to the name of the wise Yāgnyavalkya. These pieces, which were recognized by every Sanskrit scholar, on linguistic grounds, as the oldest texts of the Upanishadic literature, express a bold and rough Idealism that, even as that of the Parmenides closely related to it, contains the kernel of the eternal metaphysical truth but yet, like the latter, was no longer understood by its immediate successors and was deformed in a way that we can characterize only as a gradually increasing corruption. In doing so, the original Idealism passes over in stages to Pantheism, Cosmogonism, Theism, and finally the atheism of the Sāmkhya system and the Apsychism of the Buddhists, until the great Reformer Shankara (born 788 A.D. precisely 1000 years before Schopenhauer, spiritually related to him, and 1215 years after Plato, representing the same metaphysical fundamental principles in Greek clothing) reestablishes that original Idealism and understands the succeeding corruption of the same as an accommodation of literary exegesis to human weakness. Only that old Idealism, according to Shankara, forms the esoteric Vedānta doctrine; everything else has only an exoteric validity.

That original Idealism of Yāgnyavalkya, who has maintained, and will maintain for all time, his significance for metaphysics can be summarized in three sentences:

1. There is no other reality in the world than the ātman, that is, the Self. The husband is dear not for the sake of the husband, as Yāgnyavalkya elaborates to his wife Maitreyi, and likewise the wife, father, mother, gods, and worlds are dear not for their sake but for that of the Self. That means: the entire universe exists for me only insofar as it is present in myself, that is, in my consciousness, the universe is, as Kant would say, only an appearance, it is as Schopenhauer, strengthening the subjective aspect further, teaches, only my imagination. Therefore, one should, the Upanishad continues, see, hear and understand the Self, the ātman; one who has seen, heard and understood the ātman has therewith understood the entire universe, just as one who grasps a musical instrument has at the same time grasped the musical tones welling from it. But the following is wonderful: 'Just as a block of salt dissolved in water

makes the latter salty in all its parts, so that great, shoreless Being existing only through knowledge pervades the entire universe; it arises through these creatures and dies with them; after death there is no consciousness, I say to you.' Then spoke Maitreyi: 'My lord, you have confused me by saying that there is no consciousness after death.' But Yāgnyavalkya spoke: 'Truly I do not impart confusion; what I have said is sufficient for the understanding; for, where there is a duality as it were, one sees another, hears another, recognises another, but for one for whom everything has become his own self how should he see anybody, hear anybody, know anybody, how should he indeed know the one who knows?' In this ancient Vedic locus we see already clearly expressed what is produced as the final consequence of the Kantian-Schopenhauerian doctrine as the supreme wisdom, namely, the differentiation between the transcendental, non-spatial, non-temporal, causality-free (in common terms: ubiquitous, eternal, unchangeable) consciousness and the empirical individual consciousness that arises anew and dies away as its manifestation in every brain.[8] From this first principle are produced for Yāgnyavalkya two corollaries which take up considerable space in the Upanishads but which may be summarized briefly here:

2. The ātman, the only real Self, is 'the seer of seeing, the hearer of hearing, the knower of knowledge,' in other words, the subject of knowledge in us. That

---

[8] More details about this are to be found in the third edition of my *Elements of Metaphysics* in the preliminary Foreword : 'On the nature of Idealism', along with which, here and in what follows, my translation of *Sixty Upanishads* may be compared.

this knowing subject is still not the final one, that it is borne by the subject of the Will, which extends as the Will over the entire universe, and as non-willing may come to appearance in another divine world unknown to us, for us however becomes visible and tangible only in the phenomenon of moral action, to this last depth the Upanishadic doctrine was further developed only through the genius of Schopenhauer.[9]

3. As the subject of knowledge, the ātman is and remains forever unknowable: 'You cannot see the subject of seeing, nor hear the subject of hearing, nor know the subject of knowing through which one knows the entire world, how indeed should one know it, know the knower!' It is not through knowing that the ātman is accessible but only through a deepening into our own Self. The art of returning from the unreal external world into one's own Self and there to become aware in an immediate manner of the final secret of all existence was developed by the Indians into a complicated praxis or technique, the so-called Yoga.

The three mentioned theses of Yāgnyavalkya, the sole Reality, subjectivity, and the unknowableness of the ātman, remain for all succeeding ages as a powerful revelation but mixed by lesser thinkers with the empirical view and thereby corrupted.

The next step (which is represented by the *Chāndogya Upanishad*) can be designated, for lack of a better term, as a transition to Pantheism. The empirical external world

---

[9] [See, for instance, Arthur Schopenhauer, *The World as Will and Representation*, I, Arts.62ff.]

is real or quasi-real, and yet the sole Reality of the ātman remains valid, for this world is also the ātman: 'this is my soul in the depths of the heart, smaller than a rice grain, a millet seed, the kernel of a millet seed – this is my soul in the depths of the heart, larger than the earth, larger than the air, larger than the heavens, larger than these three worlds.'

This identification: the ātman is the universe, so often as it is represented in the Upanishads, was, however, and remains a very opaque one. Therefore one posited instead of this incomprehensible identity of the one ātman and the manifold world another paradigm of the empirical way of observation, namely Causality and, losing oneself ever more deeply, seeing things ever more obliquely, taught that the ātman as the cause brought forth this world as an effect: 'after it created this world, it entered the same (as soul).' As is evident from these words (*Taittirīya Upanishad,* 2), it is, also at this stage, which we have called Cosmogonism, nothing but the soul dwelling in me itself which (in fine accordance with Plotinus) has created the entire universe and then entered full and complete into me as my individual soul.

There follows inevitably, as a further step, (incipient in the *Kāthaka Upanishad* and perfected in the *Shvetāshvatara Upanishad*) the division into the highest world-creating ātman and the individual limited one, wherewith was reached as the final point of the development what has been the starting point for more recent philosophy, namely Theism.

But this division had to be disastrous for the following development already taking place outside the Upanishads. The world-creating ātman, after it was separated from the individual ātman and was no longer proven by it, was in general no longer satisfactorily proven anywhere in such a way as not to be thrown overboard completely by the relentlessly proliferating Realism so that one retained only a real-world (Prakriti) and the individual souls (Purusha) entrapped in it. This is the point of view of the Sāmkhya system, which develops before our eyes in the *Mahābhārata* and existing in perfect form in the *Kārikā*,[10] which can be understood only as the last product of that gradually continuing degeneration and not, as has perhaps been supposed, an original intellectual creation based on a view of Nature.

As the last step of the entire development is situated, Buddhism insofar as it adds to the atheism of Sāmkhya apsychism as well and denies the soul entirely, though only apparently since it adheres to the transmigration of souls.

Into this intellectual confusion enters, 700 years before Luther and closely related to him, the great religious and philosophical reformer Shankara. Just as Luther returns through the dimming traditions of the Middle Ages to the pure Biblical letter, so Shankara pushes aside the Sāmkhya system and Buddhism with a polemical vehemence worthy of a Luther and recognizes only the writings (*shruti*), that is, the Veda, and especially the Upanishads, as a superhuman authority. But here, he pauses and acknowledges all those earlier developmental stages, Idealism, Pantheism, Cosmogonism, and Theism, with their colorful and contradictory content, as divine expressions revealed by Brahman. From this dilemma, he found a wonderful way out that can, and perhaps will still

---

[10]   [The *Sāmkhya Kārika* of Īshvara Krishna.]

one day, serve as a model for the solution of our Christian theology. He differentiates an exoteric figurative mythical theology that is adapted to the mode of thought of the masses from the pure esoteric Vedānta doctrine, which satisfied, and even today satisfies, the strictest demands of philosophical thought. While we also refer to our *System of the Vedanta*, we wish here to highlight only the main points briefly.

The exoteric, or as Shankara says, the lower knowledge (*aparā vidyā*) leaves standing in relation to Brahman all those colorful descriptions, that is also the theistic, as accommodations to human weakness, describes the creation repeatedly emerging from Brahman in great time-cycles and adheres to the transmigration of souls which for all individual souls is without beginning and, so long as the redeeming knowledge does not enter, without end.

The redeeming knowledge is indeed constituted of the esoteric, higher knowledge (*parā vidyā*), which is consummated in the three terms of the unknowability of God, His identity with the soul, and the non-reality of the universal creation along with the transmigration of souls. These are precisely the three doctrinal terms of Yāgnyavalkya, with whom began the entire development of the Upanishads, which has, through Shankara, found its system, still predominating in India, and in the Kantian-Schopenhauerian philosophy the scientific substructure that it lacked.

******

The philosophy of the Greeks is a great, splendid whole that accompanies the Greek and, further, the Graeco-Roman world in all phases of its development for twelve hundred years, from the sixth century B.C. to the sixth century A.D., from the Seven Sages,[11] of whom Thales of Miletus was one, to the Seven Wise Men or Orphans who wandered out in 529 A.D. when Justinian, the slave of women and popes, closed the Platonic academy,[12] the last still existing, so that the Greek philosophy, like its great representative Socrates, died at an advanced age, and not through natural decay. In its long development, it counts three high points that are designated by the names of Parmenides, Plato, and Plotinus. We can ignore the last, who would only renew the doctrine of Plato and pursue it to its final finest consequences, but not Parmenides, without whom Plato cannot be understood.

At three different points of the Greek world, we see, in the sixth century B.C., when the time was ripe for it, almost at the same time, the light of philosophy shining forth in Ionian Miletus, in Dorian Kroton and Aeolian Elea (south of Naples). Of these three orientations, the actually central and by far the most significant is the philosophy of the Eleatics. Its founder Xenophanes concerned himself with theology and posited against the colorful multiplicity of the Homeric world the doctrine of the

---

[11] [The so-called Seven Sages of sixth century B.C. Greece were Thales of Miletus, Pittacus of Mytilene, Bias of Priene, Solon of Athens, Periander of Corinth or Myson of Chenae, and Chilon of Sparta.}

[12] [John Malalas, a Syrian Byzantine chronicler of the sixth century, reported in his *Chronographia* that the Christian emperor Justianian had issued a decree that aimed at closing the Platonic Academy (which was at that time Neo-Platonic rather than Platonic) at Athens and banned heretics, Jews and pagans from holding any state or educational office.]

one, unchangeable God, which is basically nothing but the unity of the universe, with the recognition of which philosophy begins here as in India.

Xenophanes was far excelled by his great pupil Parmenides, whose entire philosophy can be summarized in the phrase apparently signifying nothing: Being is, τὸ ὅν ἐστίν, (in verse ἐὸν ἔμμεναι).[13] Parmenides followed this thought and obtained through a sharp division of his subject (Being) the knowledge of the unity and, through that of his predicate (is), the knowledge of the unchangeability of Being, which can claim this name with absolute strictness. Therewith the foundations of true metaphysics were laid for all time to come and the principle of the Kantian philosophy unconsciously anticipated. For, all spatial and temporal being consists of a juxtaposition of parts, one beside, or after, the other, thus of a multiplicity, and one who denies multiplicity to Being with such sharpness as Parmenides does has denied it, also without knowing it or willing it, Space and Time, and even the occasional falling back into a quasi-spatial view when Parmenides describes his Being as 'comparable' to a ball perfectly round on all sides, cannot change anything in it. Likewise, one who has, like Parmenides, excluded change from Being has therewith also excluded the principle of differentiation, that is, Causality, from it. But not only in this principal teaching but also in the consequences of it, Parmenides accords directly with Kant. What the German thinker reaches in patient, deeply penetrating work is grasped by the Greek in a rougher and, therefore, to be sure, less effective way. With an incomparable force of abstraction, Parmenides pursues the question of how a true Being must be constituted, leaving Nature behind. After he

---

[13]   ['On Nature', 6.]

found the mentioned basic determinations of Being, he compared his thoughts on Being with Nature and found that they did not agree. Being is a unity, Nature shows us everywhere a multiplicity, Being is unchangeable, Nature is eternally changing and exchanging. And here Parmenides was great and bold enough to say to himself: If Nature does not agree with what I have found through clear and logical thought, now Nature itself is wrong, the evidence of the eyes and ears are false, the entire multiple and changeable world is based only on a false presupposition, on deceptive human opinion.

That is the form in which the great Parmenides anticipated the Kantian doctrine, that the world is only an appearance, not a thing in itself. He became thereby the father of western metaphysics, but he had to wait for more than a hundred years until the man came – who really understood him. Exactly as in India, in Greece too, the ideas of the great metaphysical genius were forced into empirical templates and thereby distorted and corrupted. The Eleatic Zeno may serve as an example. As a faithful shield-bearer of his teacher, he sought to support his ideas. Parmenides had taught that Being is one and unchangeable. Zeno undertook to show that there is no multiplicity and no change. But, alas!, he understood the metaphysical ideas of his teacher physically and undertook, quite faithfully, to prove that there is, in this empirical Reality surrounding us, no multiplicity and no change. As expected, his proofs only result in sophistries and do not deserve the esteem that has so often been granted to them.

While Parmenides followed the profound question of Being in 500 B.C. in Elea, in the farthest west of Greece there lived at the same time at the eastern border of

Greece a man who was, both geographically and in his thought the most decisive antipode of Parmenides, Heraclitus the Obscure of Ephesus. Perhaps the two did not know each other; if they had known about each other as some people, supported by a false interpretation of one passage of Parmenides' poem, suppose, they would only have abhorred each other. Just as Parmenides is a metaphysician, so Heraclitus is only a physicist. He casts an open, free glance at the empirical world surrounding him and expresses the impression it makes on him in the pregnant words: 'Everything is in flux.' Everything in Nature is caught in a continuous change, is comparable to a stream whose waves and whirls apparently remain the same but in Reality are formed from moment to moment by ever new waters. It is the law of Causality that is valid without exception in Nature, the legal necessity of becoming, that impressed itself on the investigating human mind for the first time in Heraclitus, whereas at the same time in distant Elea the same human mind established the characteristics of true Being. According to Parmenides there is only an unchangeable Being; every becoming is a mere appearance, according to Heraclitus there is only a becoming, and all lasting being is a mere appearance. In vain did the following century attempt, in Empedocles, Anaxagoras, and Democritus, to establish a reconciliation of the doctrine of Heraclitus of becoming and the not less irrefutable doctrine of Parmenides of the unchangeable Being. These philosophers too, understand Parmenides in a physical sense and explain all becoming as mere combination and decomposition of unchanging primary substances. How little their mechanical view of Nature was suited to satisfying the human mind is seen clearly in the self-disintegration of all philosophy that set in immediately after. It declares itself as the sophistry that, quite like the sophistry of our day, pays homage to the saying: 'Nothing is true, everything is permitted,' in which the doubt regarding the theoretical as well as the practical task of philosophy is clearly evident. It was opposed by Socrates, the conceptual philosopher who was concerned to find universally valid norms for knowing and acting in the power of Ideas that had been excessively overvalued by him. His influence on Plato is well-known, but less discussed and resolved is the question of whether the influence of Socrates on the Platonic genius in this direction was a beneficial one, and whether Plato's deepest impulses had not been led on a false path by Socrates. We have to concern ourselves with these now.

Permeated with the knowledge of Parmenides and not less with that of Heraclitus, Plato cast his glance at the Nature surrounding him in order to determine what the Being of Parmenides is in the Becoming of Heraclitus and what the unchangeable and lasting is in the eternal flux of things. Here he recognized that Nature, in spite of multiplicity and becoming, is not completely fluid, that, rather, in the eternal flux of appearances, certain types and forms are maintained. These are the Ideas of Plato, and they are the lasting Being of Parmenides in the contentless Becoming of Heraclitus; the two great antipodes celebrate their final reconciliation in the philosophy of Plato inspired equally by both. But it was unfortunately not granted to Plato to follow up the original view of Nature that directed him in a pure fashion. Like Kant, he too committed in the performance of his undertaking great mistakes that we must clearly designate as such if we wish to make the work of this greatest philosopher of antiquity useful for us too. What is that fundamental dogma of Plato that stays secretly in the background everywhere and from there governs his entire thought – in other words, what are the Ideas of Plato?

If we consult the usual textbooks, we find rather consistently the explanation that the Ideas of Plato are nothing but concepts, concepts imagined as objective realities, as the essences underlying all being and becoming in Nature.

This explanation of the Platonic Ideas is, superficially observed, not incorrect, and yet it is completely unsatisfactory. For, how did Plato come to the absurdity of lending to concepts, these abbreviated and faded imaginational images in the human brain, objective Reality and dominion over the Nature moving in its diamantine rocks?

As certainly as Plato, like every philosopher of first rank, was inspired and determined originally not so much by the, to be sure, easily measurable and weighable doctrinal opinions of the predecessors as rather by the imponderables that are not so easy to handle of the impression of the intuitively accessible world, so certainly must the deepest motives of Platonic thought be found in the latter. The simplistic but limited founder of the Cynical school, Antisthenes, is supposed to have said once to his classmate Plato: 'Plato, I see the horse, but I do not see Horseness (the Idea of a horse)!', to which Plato responded very trenchantly: 'You have indeed only the eyes with which one sees the horse, and you do not have the eye with which one sees horseness!' Let us hope that the eye with which one sees horseness is given to us, the metaphysical glimpse into Nature; where the latter is missing all the acumen of an Aristotle and all scholarship cannot help to understand Plato.

Whatever the Ideas of Plato may be, they are in any case, as already the ancients said, the 'unity in multiplicity,' the unity that concerns a related multiplicity as, for example, horseness is the unity that pervades and rules all individual horses of all times and countries. But what unity in multiplicity does Plato mean? There are two of them: the logical unity of the concept obtained through abstraction from appearances and the metaphysical unity of the Idea as a creating and formative force manifesting itself in individuals (in our sense, provisional to that which Plato understands by it). The Idea of the horse is, in this sense, the metaphysical unity that has not yet disintegrated through Space and Time into the multiplicity of individual horses and conditioning all in their forms and functions. The concept of the horse is the unity regained through logical abstraction from the multiplicity of individuals that is present not, like the former, in the real world but only in the human head (more details in the *Elements of Metaphysics*).

Which of these two unities does Plato mean? The answer is neither of the two because he means both of them. Unfortunately, idea and concept are blurred in his Ideas. That he has in mind concepts is proved by the majority of examples in his work (the Good, the True, the Beautiful, Identity, Difference, Justice, State, Virtue, etc.), which are all only concepts, and also by the fact that he calls the science of Ideas Dialectics and celebrates it in an effusive manner. But that Plato's Ideas, according to their original purport, are the creative natural forces is proven especially by the word Idea itself, which signifies a visible form and nothing abstract, and by the fact that he describes the Ideas in the *Phaedo* as causes, in the *Sophist* as living forces, and also by the testimony of Aristotle, who characterizes Plato's Ideas as 'eternalized sense objects' (αἰσθητὰ ἀΐδια)[14]

---

[14]   [Aristotle, *Metaphysics*, 997b.]

and repudiates them as such, though in fact, he makes available to us a most appropriate expression for what Plato's Ideas are according to their original inspiration. They are not something abstract but the concrete, universally determined, and visible forms themselves of Nature, only, as he says 'eternalized,' that is, freed of Space and Time. If we could remove Space and Time from Nature, then all individual horses divided by Space and Time would coincide into the unity of horseness, and so in all other cases. We would have removed all the appearances of inorganic and organic Nature and in their place would remain only the original types of the same as formative and efficient forces. If Plato had already had the Aristotelian logic at hand that could explain to him the true nature of the Ideas, if he had already been acquainted with modern natural science, from which he could simply read off the series of real ideas (of which we have drafted a list in the *Elements of Metaphysics*), he would have, unperturbed by the Socratean apotheosis of the concept, carried through his original intentions in a pure manner and spared the world a two thousand-year-long period of disorientation.

But perhaps we harm Plato when we criticize him for having confused ideas and concepts without distinction. One passage of his *Phaedo* (Ch.48), perhaps the most important in all of Plato, seems to make possible a yet deeper interpretation. Here Plato narrates under the persona of Socrates how, from youth on, he was imbued with the desire to see the final causes of things. 'But when I turned my glance to Nature,' he continues, 'to draw out from its confusing multiplicity those final causes, those lasting forms, I had to experience something similar to the one who looks directly into the sun and is blinded by it. But, just as he can observe the sun clothed in its rays in a mirror without danger to his eyes, so it seemed to me also necessary to resort to concepts and to regard in them (as in a mirror) the truth of Being. Perhaps we may interpret it in this manner. Plato recognized that, just as a concept corresponds to every Idea, a subjective, abstract imaginational image corresponds to every formative natural force. But Plato concluded further that just as a concept stands against every Idea, so also an Idea stands against every concept. Accordingly, he posits not only Ideas of species, horse, dog, monkey, etc., but also Ideas of all the genera as well as those of the concepts related to characteristics and relations. A horse has this or that shape and performance because it participates in the Idea of a horse. But it is, besides, an animal because it participates in the Idea of an animal and is fast because it participates in the Idea of speed. So Plato chose the concepts as guidelines to find out the Ideas; therewith, he did something superfluous insofar as the participation in the Idea of an animal, speed, etc., was already effected through the participation in the Idea of the horse containing in itself all these characteristics.

This lapse in Plato, who sought the natural forces as Ideas and apprehended them as concepts, gave rise to endless strifes, for example, in Nominalism and Realism in the Middle Ages, as well as in modern philosophy until, finally, in the philosophy of Schopenhauer the genuine Platonic Ideas emerged as an integrating part of the system and thereby could allow no further doubt about their nature and their eternal justification. And the mistake of Plato, great as it is, is also not of the sort that it could mar our joy in his Ideas or our feeling of deepest accord with him. For, by making Ideas concepts, Plato raised these logical abstractions to the dignity of efficient natural forces and enriched his Ideal world with a great number of superfluous mongrels that are, as such, easy to recognize and remove and therefore, after we have been enlightened on their nature, can cause no more great harm.

Following in the footsteps of his great teacher Parmenides, Plato differentiates two great realms, the metaphysical realm of 'the eternal Being that neither arises nor passes away,' and the physical realm of 'that which arises and passes away but is never true Being' (quote from *Timaeus*). The former includes the Ideas as the eternal archetypes of things, the latter their appearances, their imitations, reformulations, 'shadow images,' as Plato says. Indeed, when he calls his Ideas 'Being that is in itself' this expression unites the Indian term 'ātman' with the Kantian 'thing in itself, but the empirical Reality, which is explained by the Indians as mere illusion (*māyā*), by Kant as mere appearance, appears in Plato as a world of shadows. 'Think of men,' he has Socrates in the seventh book of the *Republic* say, 'as prisoners who sit chained in a cave underground in such a way that they can neither rise nor turn their head but are forced to stare at a wall surface before them. Now imagine that, behind the prisoners, a light burns and that all sorts of shapes pass by between their back and the light, then they will see neither these shapes nor the light nor even themselves but only the shadow images of all on the wall and consider these as real things.'

The interpretation of this imagery in the light of the Kantian-Schopenhauerian philosophy is easy and cannot be missed. The light is the Will as a thing-in-itself, the shapes passing by are the eternal types through which it expresses its essence in the world of appearances and which Plato sought as his Ideas and partially found; the wall stretched before us, however, is the Platonic matter that is proved in the light of the Kantian philosophy to be the interpenetration of the three subjective forms of intuition, Space, Time and Causality. And here we touch on an observation that, as little as it seems to have been employed up to now, is especially suited to bring into sharpest focus the relationship between Platonism and Kantianism.

The being that is in itself, in Plato's language the Ideas, are the only real thing in the world, and empirical things lead only a shadow existence and possess what they have of Reality on loan from the Ideas. But if that is so, how come we do not see those true realities but always only their appearances, their shadowings? On this question, we see Plato running into a great dilemma, and it is a delightful drama to see how the great philosopher struggles with this difficulty without attaining the complete clarity that only the Kantian philosophy brought to us in this question. Now we know very precisely what stands as an obscuring medium between us and the things in themselves so that we can never see the latter but always only their appearances; it is the forms innate in our intellect that force us to view that which is free of Space as spatial, that which is free of Time as temporal, that which is free of Causality as subject to the law of Causality. This answer Plato could not yet give; according to his doctrine, between our mind and the Ideas is thrust a dark something which has no reality but is still strong enough to cause that we never see the Ideas but always only their shadow images. This something is the matter that was called thus only by later Platonists. Plato does not use this expression yet; he designates it in the *Republic* as 'that which has no being,' in *Philebus* as the 'indeterminate,' but he speaks most clearly about it in *Timaeus*, which presents in very transparent mythical garb the most important information about Plato's philosophy. Here the mythical world-creator has at his disposal two essences for the world-creation, the Ideas, which Plato describes here as 'that which is identical to itself, the indivisible' and Matter, which he calls 'that which always becomes something else, the divisible.' The wonderful profundity that lies in these expressions becomes clear when we consider that Space and Time are the principles of divisibility and that Causality is the principle of changeableness, all three of which are thus removed by Plato from the Ideas and directed to matter. The demiurge creates out of Ideas and Matter first a middle, mixed entity and spreads further all three, the Idea, the Mixed, and Matter, onto the soul, first the world-soul, and builds within the latter the body of the world that he derives from Matter. The description of this causes the philosopher great difficulty; it has, he says, 'a share in the spiritual in a quite incomprehensible manner,' it is understandable only through a certain false syllogism.[15]

In the further representation of Matter there is evident in Plato a real wavering, and the interpreters argue about whether Plato's Matter is the substance divested of all qualities or if it is mere Space. Both interpretations can appeal to Plato's representation, and especially his vacillation on this point is proof of his higher philosophical discretion. If I take a body and deduct from it everything real, idea-like, then everything that I see, hear, touch, smell, and taste in it, to the extent to which I do this the body will gradually disappear, and the moment I remove from it the final force and qualitative aspect and, in Plato's language, the last share that it has in

---

[15] The explanation of this mysterious expression I have given in my *Commentatio de Platonis Sophista*, Bonn, 1869, pp.32-34.

the world of Ideas, the entire body will disappear and only the empty space that it filled remain. Bodies are, in Kant's correct definition, 'force-filled spaces,' they are, in Plato's view, a matter filled with Ideational elements that would in this respect be only mere space, as Plato occasionally designates it. On the other hand, we have the feeling that, even when we deduct from a body all qualities, everything resembling force and Ideas, still something else remains than mere space, so to speak, a dark, blurry mass which, after the deduction of all qualities, is, to be sure, neither visible nor tangible nor apprehensible in any other way, but yet poses itself as a certain something to our imaginational powers. It is this substance fully free of qualities of which Schopenhauer has shown in a brilliant way that it is only the objective reflection of Causality representing itself in Space and Time, that it, in other words, is only the interpenetration of the three subjective forms of intuiting – Space, Time, and Causality.

We see Plato on the way to this knowledge when he deals with his Matter, sometimes as mere Space, sometimes as a substance free of qualities. To the graphically inclined Greek adhering to vision, to whom the unknowable thing in itself is represented in a knowable form as the world of Ideas, matter too had to appear as something if not real yet as something quasi-real. As such, it poses resistance to his critical thought, and it was reserved only to Kant, the incomparable analytical thinker, to overcome this phantom by dissolving the substance free of qualities into the forms of knowledge innate and inherent in our intellect – Space, Time, and Causality.

*****

In all countries and in all ages, in near and distant lands, it is the same Nature of things that faces the same observing mind. How could it be otherwise than that the thinking mind, insofar as it is not deluded by traditions and prejudices, insofar as it confronts Nature purely and objectively, should in its research into it reach the same results everywhere, in India as in Greece, in ancient as in modern times! We have compared the three brilliant manifestations of philosophy, the Vedānta, Plato, and Kant. We have not twisted and quibbled, bent and circumvented, but we have allowed every appearance to appear in its complete individual character. But by penetrating to the final depths in the case of each of them, we have reached the inner starting point from which the views of the Indian, Greek, and German thinkers arose and this inner concord along with differences in external aspect is not a small guarantee that we perceive in all three the voice of the one Nature agreeing with itself, that we perceive in them the voice of eternal Truth.

Belief is outdated, doubt is modern and fashionable, and yet the skepticism of our days gnawing at everything and unable to offer any true satisfaction has not been able to prevent old crude superstition from raising its wild head again. Between the two, and through them, unperturbed, goes the knowledge of Truth on its quiet, sure way. And even if its voice is temporarily drowned by the noise of fashionable follies, it still remains undeterred. A better future will grant it what the present denies it. It can wait, because it has a long life, it is eternal.